Are you scared of thunder?

CURIOUS
Questions & answers about...

Weather

Do you prefer hot or cold weather?

Where do you live on planet Earth?

What name would you give to a hurricane?

Where would you go on an adventure?

What do you do to have fun?

Words by Philip Steele

Illustrations by Mike Moran

Miles Kelly

What is weather?

Earth is surrounded by a layer of air called the atmosphere. The way the atmosphere behaves is always changing. It is these changes that give us the weather, which may be hot, cold, wet, windy or sunny.

Sun

The atmosphere is filled with moving air and clouds

Mind the wind doesn't blow your hat off!

Earth

South Pole

Why does weather happen?

The Sun is the nearest star to Earth. It is far, far away in space, but its incredible heat warms our planet. This warmth affects the way that air presses against Earth's surface. Differences between cold and warm places create strong winds, as well as currents in the oceans.

Why do seasons change?

As Earth travels around the Sun, it is tilted. This means that northern and southern parts lean towards to the Sun at different times of the year. So when the north part is leaning towards the Sun it is summer there, and winter in the southern part.

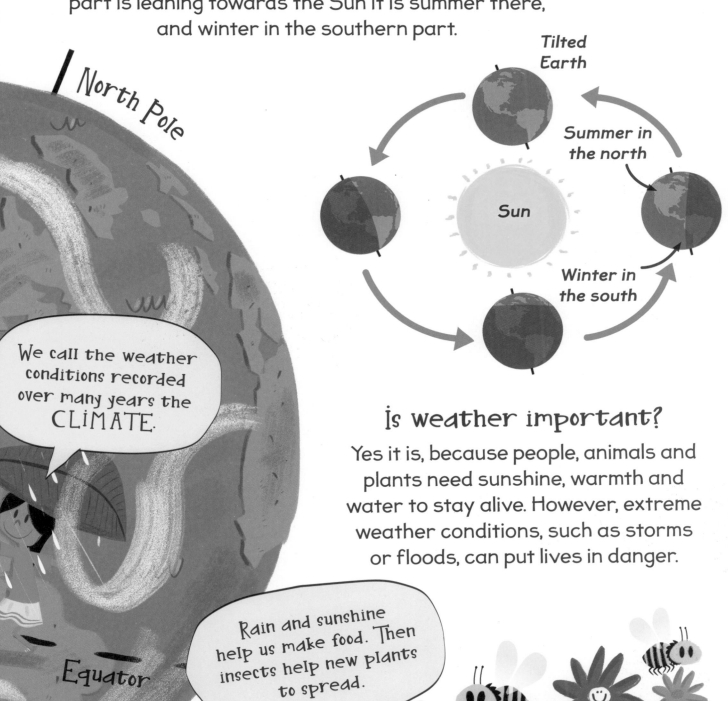

Tilted Earth

Summer in the north

Sun

Winter in the south

North Pole

We call the weather conditions recorded over many years the CLIMATE.

Equator

Is weather important?

Yes it is, because people, animals and plants need sunshine, warmth and water to stay alive. However, extreme weather conditions, such as storms or floods, can put lives in danger.

Rain and sunshine help us make food. Then insects help new plants to spread.

What makes water wonderful?

Water is a liquid. It can freeze to become solid ice. It can turn into a gas called water vapour. Water may change its form, but it lasts forever.

2 It gets gassy

Heat from the Sun turns water into a gas, called water vapour. This is **evaporation**.

1 There's lots of it!

Over **two thirds** of the Earth's surface is covered in water.

Water is precious

Fresh water keeps us **alive**. Water helps plants grow, too. We can wash in it, swim in it, sail on it, and play in it!

Whoosh! Splash!

3 It rises and cools

As warm water vapour rises, it cools down. It **condenses**, turning back into liquid.

The higher you go, the colder it gets!

4 It makes clouds

Water droplets or solid ice crystals gather around specks of dust and form **clouds**.

5 It falls back down

Don't forget your umbrella!

Water droplets or ice crystals form **raindrops** or **snowflakes**, which fall back to Earth.

6 It goes on and on

Rain and melted snow fill rivers, lakes and oceans, then the whole **water cycle** starts all over again. It helps create our weather.

How hot does it get?

In California's Death Valley, the top temperature ever recorded was over 56°C. A weather satellite has recorded over 70°C in the Lut Desert in Iran.

Where is the driest place on Earth?

The Atacama Desert in Chile. Once, no rain fell there for over 14 years. Long periods without rain are called droughts.

We can measure temperature in degrees Celsius (°C). At the centre of the Sun it's about 15 million°C.

Why do lizards sunbathe?

Reptiles such as lizards are cold-blooded, which means that they can't make their own heat. They bask in the sunshine to warm themselves up.

Atacama Desert

Lizard

How can plants survive in a desert?

Some plants have their own water supply. Cacti store water in their thick, spiky stems. Baobab trees store water inside their big, fat trunks.

Cactus

Baobab tree

Why can the Sun be a danger?

The Sun can burn your skin and make you ill. On a sunny day, cover up your skin, wear a hat, slap on some sun cream and drink plenty of water.

Don't forget I need a drink too!

Where does the weather happen?

In the layer of the atmosphere that is closest to Earth's surface. The atmosphere surrounds our planet like a giant blanket, screening out some harmful rays that come from the Sun.

Atmosphere

Cumulonimbus

What is a weather system?

Huge masses of air that swirl over Earth's surface are called weather systems. High pressure systems press air down against the land. They bring drier, clearer weather. Low pressure systems bring mild or rainy weather. The border between two systems is called a front.

On TV, the weather is explained with maps and symbols.

Cirrus

Why do clouds have funny shapes?

Some clouds are white and puffy, some are thin and streaky. Some pile up like big dark towers, some form little blobs. Their shape depends on whether they are full of water droplets or ice crystals and how high up they are.

Mackerel sky

Some clouds look like dragons, castles or bears in the sky. What can you see up there?

Is there a pot of gold at the end of a rainbow?

Only in fairy tales! Rainbows are the most beautiful sights in the sky. Air has no colour, but when sunlight passes through rain or mist, the water droplets break up the light into an arc of shimmering colours.

Why does the wind blow?

Because as warm air rises, cold air whooshes in to take its place, and the wind blows! Some winds blow between land and sea. Some cross deserts and mountains. Others blow all the way around the planet.

Cold air

Warm air

Sycamore seeds

How does the wind help plants?

Many trees and flowering plants have seeds that are scattered by the wind. Dandelion seeds are light and fluffy, and float a long way. Sycamore seeds are like helicopter blades, spinning around.

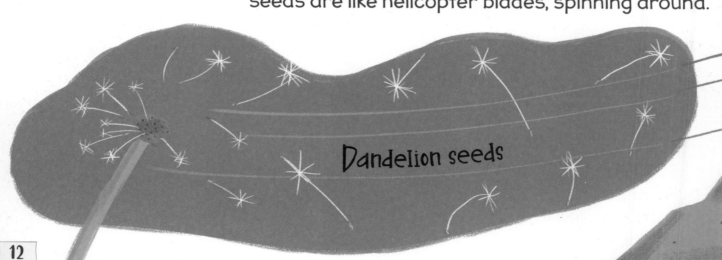

Dandelion seeds

What is the monsoon?

It is a wind that blows across India. The winter monsoon brings dry weather. In summer it picks up lots of water from the ocean and brings heavy rains to the dry land.

Summer monsoon can bring flooding.

Wandering albatross

Condor

Why do birds ride on the wind?

So we can fly long distances without too much flapping. Over the Southern Ocean, albatrosses like me glide on powerful winds. In South America, condors use currents of warm air to soar above mountains.

Pillar

How do winds shape rock?

Winds often carry dust, grit or sand. They blast rocks and cliffs, wearing them down into all sorts of shapes. Water, ice and heat also shape the surface of planet Earth.

Arch

Would you rather?

Go on holiday somewhere **cold** or somewhere **hot**?

Hear crashing **thunder** or see flashes of **lightning**?

BANG!

FLASH!

Play football in the **rain and mud** or during a **heatwave**?

Cruise by boat on a **calm day**...

...or sail on a **windy day**?

Fly **above** the clouds...

Sheep's wool contains lanolin, a grease that keeps out the rain.

Wear a **woolly coat** like a sheep, or a **green raincoat** like a tree frog?

I am covered in waterproof skin!

Ride on a **surfboard**...

...or a **snowboard**?

Work outside in a **big storm** at sea or inside designing a weather satellite for space?

...or drift **below** the clouds?

What is a hurricane?

It's a terrifying tropical storm, also called a typhoon or a cyclone. A great storm cloud spins around as it sweeps over the ocean. Hurricane-force winds can reach 180 kilometres an hour or even more.

The calm centre is called the 'eye' of the storm.

Is it deadly?

When a hurricane smashes into land it can be deadly. There are huge waves, heavy rain, floods and mudslides. Trees can be blown over, homes may be destroyed, and lives may be at risk.

Where is Tornado Alley?

This is an area in the United States that has some of the fiercest whirlwinds of all. They are called tornadoes or twisters. These dark funnels of dust can spin at up to 500 kilometres an hour. They can suck up a car or even a house.

WATCH OUT!

What is a waterspout?

A whirlwind that forms from warm, moist air over a sea or lake is called a waterspout. It is often joined to the bottom of a cloud.

Why are thunder clouds dark?

Thunder clouds are so full of water droplets that they look very dark. They tower up to 15 kilometres high.

How do clouds make lightning?

Water vapour rushes up into clouds from the warm ground. Once inside, the vapour cools and freezes, forming balls of ice called hailstones. Air currents ping these up and down inside the cloud, making an electric charge.

In a thunderstorm, stay away from water or metal fences.

BANG!

BOOM!

Why does thunder go bang?

The heat of lightning is incredible, even hotter than the Sun. It makes the air expand so fast that it causes a shockwave. BANG!

Which comes first, thunder or lightning?

They happen at the same time, but we see the flash first because light travels through the air faster than sound.

Thunderstorms can be dangerous.

How fast is lightning?

The electricity connects with the ground or with other clouds, forming a flash of lightning. This can travel 120,000 kilometres in a single second.

Go indoors if you can.

Do not stand under a tree.

Did you know?

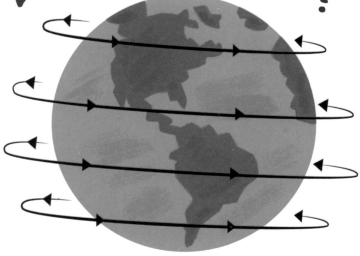

Super-powerful long-distance winds called **jet streams** rip along about 10 kilometres above the Earth's surface.

The Inuit people of the Arctic can build **igloos** — overnight shelters made from blocks of frozen snow. These are actually quite cosy!

It is said that no two **snowflakes** have exactly the same design!

Fog is just low-level cloud. The Grand Banks off Newfoundland, Canada, have about 206 foggy days each year.

As you are reading these words, there are about 2000 **thunderstorms** happening around the world.

The spinning of the Earth forces **winds** that blow from the Poles to the Equator to change direction.

COUGH!

When fumes from cars and factories react with sunlight, the air is filled with horrible, poisonous **smog**.

The coats of the **Arctic fox** and **hare** change to white in the winter, so they cannot be seen against the snow.

Fir trees have thin, tough leaves called **needles**, which stay on all winter. These help capture sunlight all year round. They can store water and survive harsh winter storms.

Long ago, people believed that the weather was controlled **by gods and goddesses**. Inti was the Inca Sun god. Thor was the Norse god of thunder.

How are snowflakes formed?

When water droplets freeze around specks of dust in a cloud, snowflakes form. These ice crystals freeze more droplets, building up amazing starry shapes and patterns. They stick together to make bigger flakes.

Snowflakes have SIX sides, or points.

What is a blizzard?

A blizzard is a heavy snow storm driven by high winds. Snow piles up in deep drifts. It's hard to see where you are going as everything looks white!

Why are mountaintops snowy?

Mountaintops are often covered in snow, even in hot countries. The higher you climb, the more the air expands and cools. This leads to more moisture — and snowy mountain conditions.

Where does frost make flowers?

On cold surfaces such as windows, ice or rock. Ice crystals spread into beautiful patterns, which look like ferns or flowers.

Does the sea ever freeze?

Yes it does, but because the sea contains salt, it has a lower freezing point. It turns to ice below -2° Celsius. Freshwater rivers and lakes freeze at 0° Celsius.

DANGER THIN ICE!

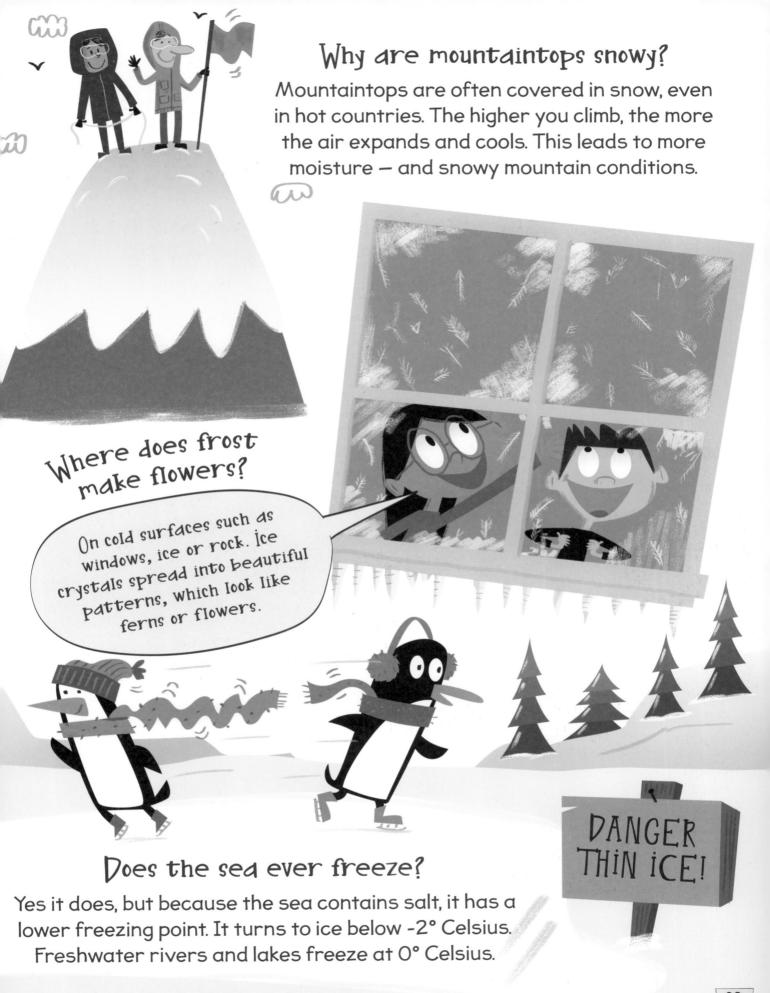

How many?

The number of days it once rained non-stop on the Hawaiian Island of Oahu!

332

4000
The number of hours of sunshine that Yuma, Arizona, USA receives in a year. It may be the sunniest place on Earth!

The biggest tropical storm ever recorded was a typhoon named Tip, in 1979. It measured **2220** kilometres across.

5 years!

That's how long a water-holding frog can go without water during a drought!

11.5 metres: The amount of snow that fell at Tamarack in California, USA, during just one day in 1911.

321
The number of kilometres a single lightning streak ran across the sky above Oklahoma, USA in 2007.

207
The number of tornadoes that happened in a single day in the USA in 2011.

8 hours **58** minutes:
The longest-lasting rainbow in Taiwan, in 2017.

−89.2° Celsius.
The lowest temperature ever recorded was at the Vostok scientific base in Antarctica, in July 1983.

1
The weight in kilograms of giant hailstones that fell in Bangladesh in 1986.

BRRRR!

How do we measure the weather?

All sorts of clever gadgets have been invented over the years to measure how the weather behaves. Today, the numbers are often recorded and displayed digitally.

Anemometers measure wind speed. They are often fixed to tall buildings, bridges and ships.

Rain gauges collect and measure the amount of rain that falls into a jar.

Thermometers measure how hot or cold it gets. The best known thermometers show how a liquid metal called mercury goes up or down inside a glass tube. Most weather scientists today use electrical resistance thermometers.

Barometers measure changes in air pressure. There are many different designs and displays.

Satellites

Weather balloons carry instruments high above Earth to study the atmosphere.

Satellites in space help us collect information about the climate. Buoys and ships at sea also record weather data, and so do aircraft.

Buoy

Weather science is called meteorology.

Does the climate ever change?

Over millions of years, Earth's climate has gone through many changes. In the past there have been great ice ages, when ice spread out from the poles.

I lived in the ice age thousands of years ago.

Woolly mammoth

What's happening today?

The climate is changing very quickly. This is because we are cutting down forests and burning too much oil, gas and coal. We are filling the atmosphere with gases that make the planet overheat.

Solar panels use energy from the Sun to create electricity

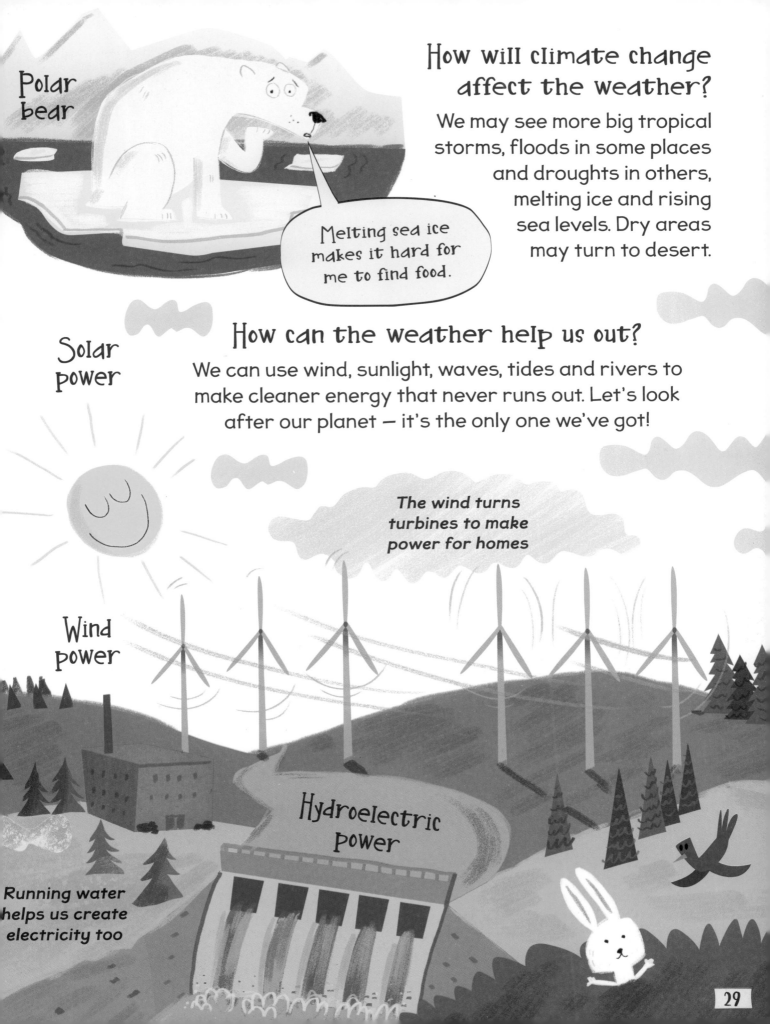

Polar bear

Melting sea ice makes it hard for me to find food.

How will climate change affect the weather?

We may see more big tropical storms, floods in some places and droughts in others, melting ice and rising sea levels. Dry areas may turn to desert.

How can the weather help us out?

We can use wind, sunlight, waves, tides and rivers to make cleaner energy that never runs out. Let's look after our planet – it's the only one we've got!

Solar power

The wind turns turbines to make power for homes

Wind power

Hydroelectric power

Running water helps us create electricity too

A compendium of questions

Why is rain sometimes red?

If rain gets mixed with sand picked up by desert winds, it can be red or orange.

Hi, i'm Katrina!

Hi, i'm Mitch!

Why are hurricanes given names?

It's an easy way of remembering which was which. Famous tropical storms have been called Katrina, Maria, Mitch and David.

Why do crocodiles like tropical storms?

If it floods, crocodiles can go hunting in the high street. You'd better watch out!

Where is there a special snow festival?

It is held each year in Sapporo, Japan. People make amazing statues and sculptures from ice and snow.

Why do people build houses on stilts?

When it floods in the rainy season in Assam, India, the houses stay high and dry.